Looking after the egg

CONTENTS

Introduction.. 2

Winter eggs..3

    Laying the egg.......................................5

    Carrying the egg....................................6

    The females leave................................. 8

    Keeping warm.....................................10

Spring chicks... 14

    Hatching..14

    The females return............................. 15

Conclusion... 18

Index... 20

Introduction

Emperor penguins are the largest penguins in the world. They are about as tall as a seven-year-old child. But they are much heavier.

Emperor penguins are 1.15 metres tall. They weigh 40 kilograms.

Emperor penguins live in the coldest, windiest place on Earth. They live in the **Antarctic**.

Winter eggs

Emperor penguins lay their eggs in winter. All the other penguins living in the Antarctic lay their eggs in spring.

Adélie

Gentoo

Chinstrap

Macaroni

King

Emperor

Six species of penguin lay their eggs and bring up their chicks in the Antarctic.

Winter in the Antarctic is extremely cold. Freezing winds blow across the ice. In the middle of winter, it is dark all day as well as all night.

At the beginning of winter, the surface of the sea
freezes into ice. Emperor penguins always come back
to the same place. They stand on the frozen sea and
call to each other.

Laying the egg

The female lays one egg. She puts the egg on her feet. The egg must not stay on the ice. The ice would freeze the egg very quickly. The male takes the egg from the female and puts it on to his feet.

13 cm long

Hen's egg

Emperor penguin's egg

Carrying the egg

Emperor penguins do not build nests. The male carries the egg on his feet instead. He tucks the egg under a special fold of skin. The egg keeps warm against his body.

brood pouch

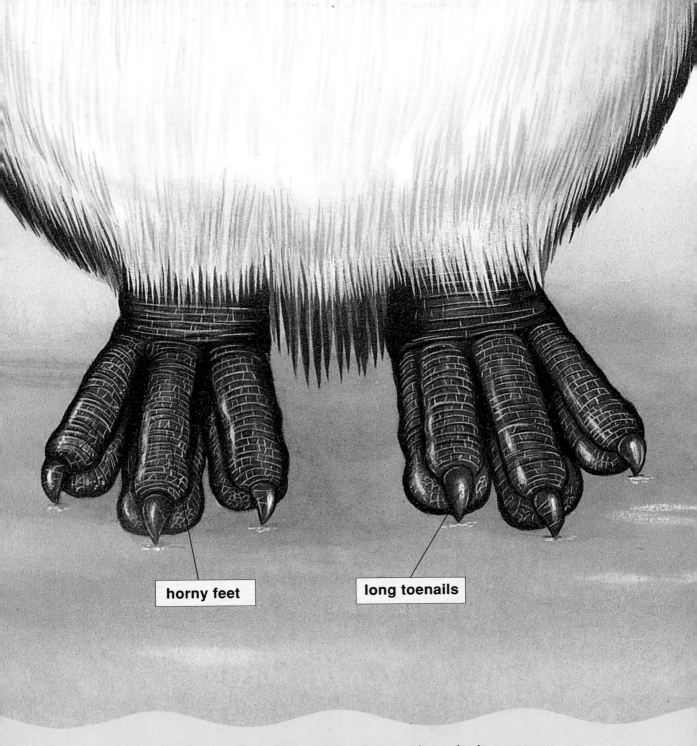

horny feet

long toenails

Emperor penguins have long toenails to help grip on to the slippery ice. Their feet are covered with hard and horny skin.

The females leave

The penguins' food is in the sea. But the sea is a long way away across the ice.

The female Emperor penguins are very hungry. Egg laying uses up a lot of energy. They must go to the sea and find food.

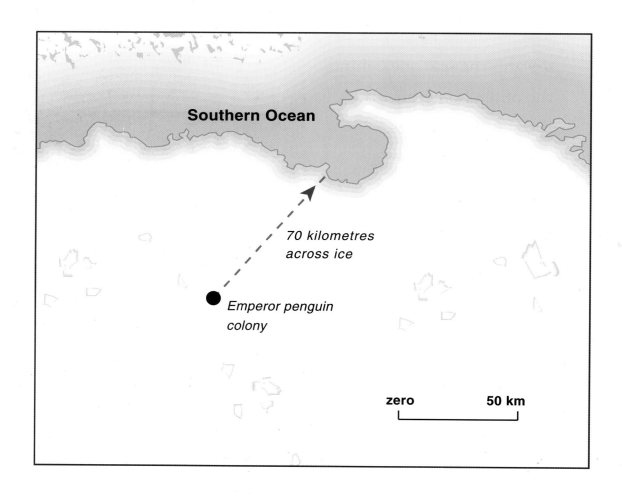

Southern Ocean

70 kilometres across ice

Emperor penguin colony

zero   50 km

The female penguins walk towards the sea, one behind the other. Sometimes they slide on their bellies, pushing with their feet.

When they reach the open sea they dive in and begin hunting for food. Every day they swim and eat.

Penguins have black backs and white bellies. This helps them to hide in the sea from their enemies.

Keeping warm

The male Emperor penguins stand on the ice looking after the eggs.

They stand day after day, week after week. It is dark. In the middle of winter the sun never rises. The only light comes from the moon, and the stars.

When cold winds blow the penguins stand very still. They hunch their heads down into their shoulders to keep warm. They have a thick layer of fat under their skin. It helps protect them from the cold. Their feathers are waterproof and windproof to help keep out the cold.

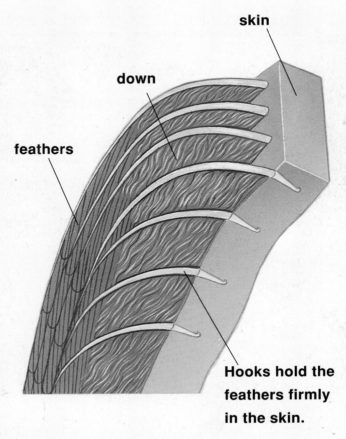

Emperor penguins have four layers of feathers to protect them from cold.

skin

down

feathers

Hooks hold the feathers firmly in the skin.

Terrible storms called **blizzards** howl across the ice.
The penguins stand as close as they can, leaning on
each other. They pack tightly together into a huge
huddle. They help each other to stay warm.

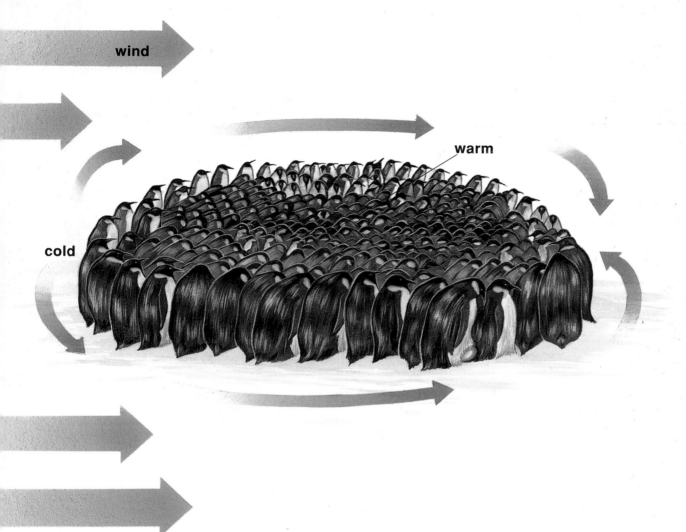

wind

warm

cold

Inside the huddle the penguins change places with each other. Every penguin gets a chance to be warm in the middle of the huddle.

Walking is very difficult for the male penguins because they have eggs on their feet. They shuffle very slowly around the huddle.

Spring chicks

Hatching

After 65 days the chick hatches. It must not stand on the ice. It would freeze to death in two minutes. The chick stands on the male's feet. It keeps warm under the fold of skin.

The males feed the chicks with special food from their gullets. But they can only do this for a few days. They wait for the females to come back.

The females return

The female Emperor penguins walk back from the sea just after the chicks hatch.

There are thousands of Emperor penguins on the ice. The males and females must find each other. Each pair of penguins has a special call. They call to each other in the crowd.

The female has plenty of food to give the hungry little chick. She takes the chick from the male. She puts the chick on her feet, under the fold of skin.

The male penguins have not eaten for nearly four months. They are very thin and tired and hungry. Now they can begin walking to the sea.

The female bends down and sings to the chick on her feet. The chick bobs its head up and down and whistles back. They must learn each other's calls so that later on they can find each other.

After three weeks the male comes back from the sea. Now he looks after the chick while the female walks back to the sea to find food.

Conclusion

Emperor penguins lay their eggs in winter so that the chicks can hatch in spring. This gives the chicks as much time as possible to grow big and strong before winter comes again.

The chick stays in the pouch for about two months.

The chicks are three months old. They rest after a big meal.

At five months the chicks develop adult feathers.

Emperor penguins have to work hard to look after their chicks. Only about half the chicks survive this first hard year of life.

Index

Antarctic.................................. **2, 3**

blizzard................................... **12**

brood pouch............................ **6**

call..................................... **4, 15, 17**

feathers.................................. **11**

food........................**8, 9, 14, 16, 17**

horny feet.............................. **7**

huddle...................................**12, 13**

skin...................................... **11**

toenails................................. **7**

winter................................... **10**